DISCOVER  SCIENCE
STRUCTURE

Kim Taylor

Chrysalis Children's Books

DISCOVER SCIENCE

Contents

First published in the UK in 2003 by
Chrysalis Children's Books
An imprint of Chrysalis Books Group Plc, The Chrysalis Building, Bramley Road London W10 6SP

Paperback edition first published in 2005

Copyright © Chrysalis Books Group Plc
Text © Kim Taylor Times Four Publishing Ltd
Photographs © Kim Taylor and Jane Burton
(except where credited elsewhere)

ISBN 1 84138 621 9 (hb)
ISBN 1 84458 450 X (pb)

Designed by Tony Potter, Times Four Publishing Ltd

Illustrated by Guy Smith

Science adviser: Richard Oels, Warden Park School, Cuckfield, Sussex

Printed in China

About this book

This book contains many fascinating photographs to help you learn about structure – the shapes and forms of things. For example, you can find out about the structure of animal and plant cells, crystals, skeletons and honeycombs, and you can discover how people have copied some of these natural shapes.

Each topic has a simple experiment for you to try. These will help you have fun while finding out more about the structure of things, from a sugar crystal to the shell of a prawn. You can even discover how to tell the age of a fish!

Domes are very strong structures. This dome is at the Epcot Centre, Florida, USA.

Crystals

Everything you can touch and feel is made up of **atoms**. Atoms are so small that you cannot see them. The tiniest speck of soot is made of billions of atoms of **carbon**. Atoms of one sort can join with atoms of another sort to make a compound. The smallest particle of a compound is called a **molecule**. A water molecule is made of one atom of oxygen (O) joined to two atoms of hydrogen (H_2). That is why the scientific name for water is H_2O. Molecules in a liquid can move around. But in a solid material they have fixed positions from which they cannot move. Instead, they vibrate. Some **crystals** are formed of neatly stacked layers of molecules.

Crystal shapes

Crystals grow when a liquid **evaporates** from a **solution**, or when a liquid freezes into a solid. They can even form from vapour. Frost is ice crystals formed from water vapour in the air. The shape of a crystal depends on how the molecules that make it up are arranged.

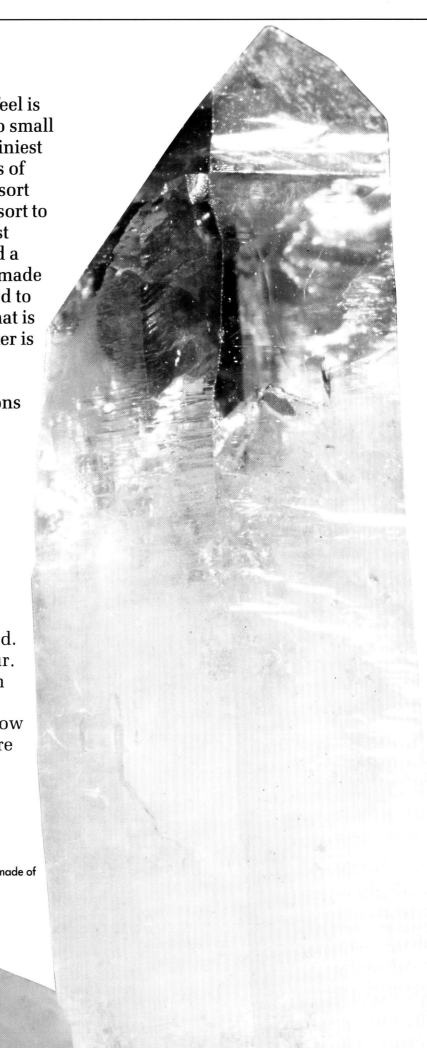

This amethyst crystal is made of silica.

Frost on a fallen leaf. Frost crystals form when water vapour in the air freezes.

Structure experiment

CRYSTALLIZED

1 Put 2 or 3 pinches of sugar in ¼ of an eggcupful of warm water. Stir and leave until dissolved.

2 Put a few droplets of the sugar water on to the mirror and leave them to dry.

3 When the droplets are dry, crystals will form. You can see them through a magnifying glass. Do they look like the sugar crystals in the photograph below?

4 Try the experiment again using salt instead of sugar.

You need
- A pocket mirror
- Sugar
- An eggcup
- Water
- A magnifying glass

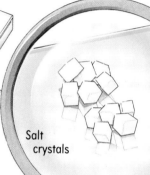

Salt crystals

Liquid or solid?

Water is a liquid because its molecules can move about. Ice is a solid because its molecules are fixed in neat layers. Sometimes it is difficult to know whether something is a liquid or a solid. Pitch is a hard, black substance. You can easily smash it into bits. But if you left some for a long time in a can with a hole in the bottom, the pitch would slowly ooze out.

Let a drop of sugar solution dry up and crystals will form. They show different colours when polarized light is shone through them.

Cells

A cell is a very small space, usually only big enough to hold one object. There are cells in the seed heads of some plants. Each cell may have just enough room for one seed. Bees and wasps build cells, one for each of their larvae to grow in. All plants and animals are made up of **microscopic** cells. These cells have a very thin, tough outer skin with the living part inside. The living part is called cytoplasm and looks like a thick liquid with particles in it. The largest and most important particle in the cell is the **nucleus**. Each cell has one nucleus that controls all the activity inside it.

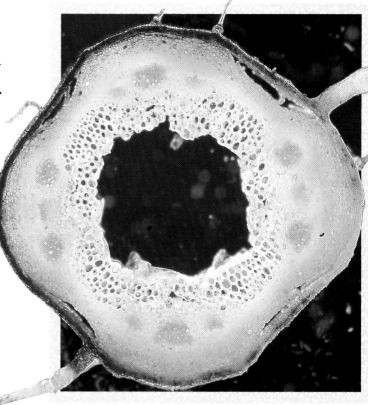

A thin slice cut across a stinging nettle stem shows that it is made of different kinds of cells. Each stinging hair is a single cell.

Dividing cells

When plants and animals grow, their cells do not get bigger. Instead, the cells divide to make more cells. In plants, the nucleus first splits in half to make two nuclei. Then gradually a cell wall forms between the nuclei, so that one cell becomes two. Protozoa are the smallest animals that exist. They consist of only one cell and reproduce (make a new protozoon) by splitting in half.

These long-shaped protozoa are darting about in pond water. They are so small that you can only just see them with your naked eye.

Sunflower seeds grow inside cells in the flower head. The cells are arranged in a complicated spiral pattern.

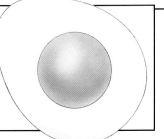

Structure experiment

FROM SEED TO CELL!

You need
- Three or four sunflower seeds
- A large flower pot with soil in
- Water

1 In early summer, plant the seeds about 2cm deep in the pot of soil.

2 Water the seeds well. After the seedlings appear be sure to water them regularly.

3 By the end of the summer the plant will grow quite tall. It will flower and produce seeds. Look at the seeds, each in its own cell. Study the pattern in the seed head.

Honeycomb

The cells made by bees and wasps have six sides. Six-sided cells fit together neatly and waste less space than cells with four sides. Imagine a round bee larva in a square cell. The corners of the cell would be wasted space. Round cells packed together would also leave gaps between them.

Inside a beehive, worker bees store honey in neat rows of cells.

Plant skeletons

Plants need tough skeletons inside them to help them stand up. Their skeletons are not rigid like bones, but bend so that the plants can sway in the wind. Plant skeletons are made up of fibres, which are very fine strands of tough material. The stalks of plants often have bundles of fibres around the outside and are hollow in the middle like tubes. A tubular stalk is stronger than a solid one of the same weight (see p.18). Even leaves have a tough skeleton, as you can see in the picture on the right.

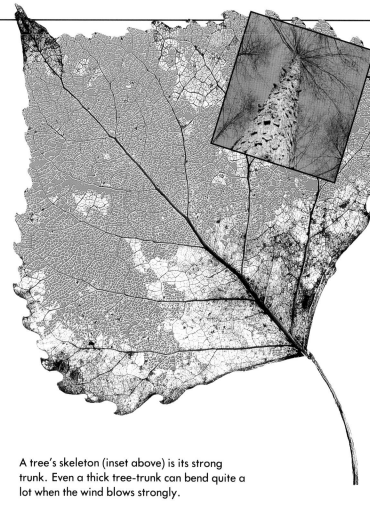

A tree's skeleton (inset above) is its strong trunk. Even a thick tree-trunk can bend quite a lot when the wind blows strongly.

Spinning a thread

Plant fibres can be very strong. Cotton thread is made by spinning together the fibres which surround the cotton seeds. Linen fabric is made from the fibres in the stem of a small plant called flax. Artificial fibres, like nylon, are mixed with plant fibres to make hardwearing fabric for clothes. Rope is often made from tough plant fibres twisted or braided together. Nylon and other artificial fibres make the strongest rope.

The rope used in this tug-of-war (right) is made of tough plant fibres. It is so strong that it will not break, however hard the people pull.

8

The soft green stalks of bluebells have a skeleton of fibres inside them. When the bluebells die, they leave behind their dry skeletons.

Structure experiment

SPOT THE SKELETON

You need

- A stalk of celery with leaves.
- Dark blue or red ink
- A glass jar
- A knife

1 Carefully cut about 2cm from the bottom of the stalk of celery.

2 Put 5cm of ink into the jar and stand the stalk of celery in it.

3 Leave the celery in the ink for a few hours, until you see the ink in the leaf veins at the top of the stalk.

4 Take the celery out of the ink and wash it. You will be able to see the tubes of the plant's skeleton stained by the ink.

Animal skeletons

Most animals have a skeleton of some kind to support and protect their bodies. **Muscles** are attached to the skeleton to make parts of it move so that the animal can walk, swim or fly. The skeleton also protects important parts of the animal, such as its brain and heart. Insects and some animals such as crabs have hard outer skeletons. Other animals, such as fish and mammals, have a bony skeleton inside them. Some undersea sponges have skeletons made of **silica**, which is the same chemical as glass. A few animals have no skeletons, including jellyfish and octopuses.

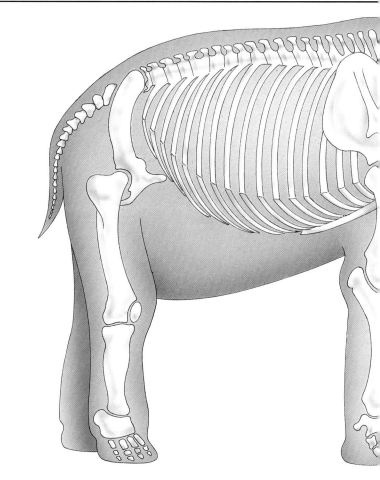

Pushing and pulling

Two main forces keep a bridge upright. **Compression** forces, which push, and **tension** forces which pull. The parts of a bridge under compression must be thick and rigid. The parts under tension are thinner and more flexible. An elephant's legs have bones that are thick and rigid. They carry its weight and are under compression. The ligaments along its backbone are under tension. They are thin, flexible and tough.

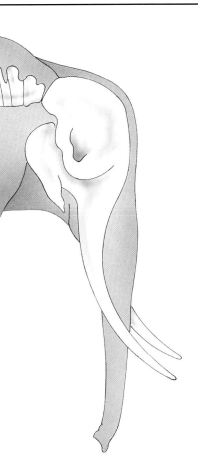

An elephant's skeleton has to support a very heavy body. Here you can see how its skeleton is constructed.

Structure experiment

SKELEFANT!

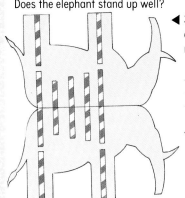

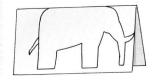
1 Fold the tracing paper in half. Trace the elephant opposite with the fold of the paper along its back.

2 Cut round the elephant's tail, legs, ▶ body and head. Leave its back uncut. Does the elephant stand up well?

◀ **3** Open out the elephant shape. Cut drinking straws and glue them on to make a backbone, ribs and leg bones.

4 Fold the elephant back together. Glue the halves of its trunk and tail together. Glue on ears. Does it stand up better now? Why?
▼

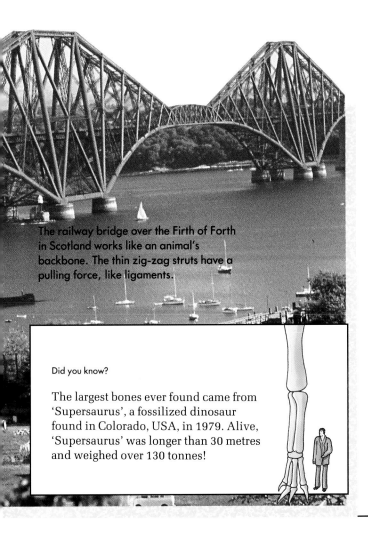

The railway bridge over the Firth of Forth in Scotland works like an animal's backbone. The thin zig-zag struts have a pulling force, like ligaments.

Did you know?

The largest bones ever found came from 'Supersaurus', a fossilized dinosaur found in Colorado, USA, in 1979. Alive, 'Supersaurus' was longer than 30 metres and weighed over 130 tonnes!

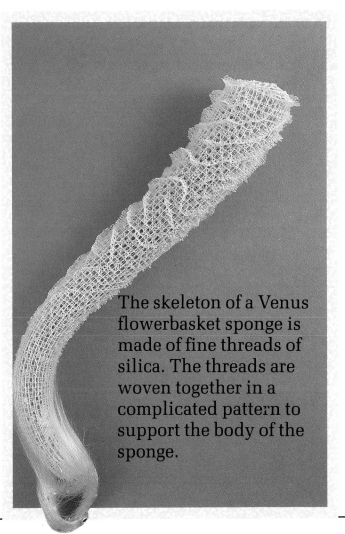

The skeleton of a Venus flowerbasket sponge is made of fine threads of silica. The threads are woven together in a complicated pattern to support the body of the sponge.

Armour

Insects and some marine animals, such as crabs and lobsters, have a hard, bony covering on the outside of their soft bodies. This outer skeleton means that they are well protected from harm. But, like a suit of armour, an outer skeleton is heavy and contains complicated joints to help the animal move. Animals with outer skeletons generally cannot move as freely or as quickly as animals with skeletons inside their bodies.

Structure experiment

PRAWN CRACKERS!

1 Bend the prawn with its shell on. You will find that it bends easily only where the sections of its shell meet.

2 Bend the prawn back against its natural curve until you hear a snapping sound.

3 Pull the prawn out of its shell. How does the body bend now? Notice how the shell feels.

You need

- A cooked, unpeeled prawn (the larger the better).
- Clean hands

A new suit

An animal stuck inside its armour cannot grow. So a new skin grows beneath the outer armour. The old armour splits open and the animal steps out in a soft new suit, one size larger. After an hour or two, the new suit has hardened into tough new armour.

A cockroach that has just shed its skin is soft and white. In a few hours, the new skin will harden and turn brown.

Insects take a few minutes to change their skins. Shrimps take only seconds. But the animal that emerges is soft and easy prey. That is why animals often hide away to change their armour.

Armour plating

Most outer skeletons are made of a very tough material called **chitin**. Chitin is springy but does not stretch. The skeletons of lobsters and crabs are rigid because the chitin is strengthened with **calcium carbonate**. The armour worn by medieval knights was made of steel, which is much tougher than chitin. An outer skeleton, like steel armour, needs to be formed of many jointed sections so that its occupant can move.

Knights in armour are protected against injury, but their armour is heavy and they cannot move fast.

Shells

Some animals have a shell for protection. A shell is different from an outer skeleton because it does not cover an animal's body like a skin. It is more like a home that the animal carries around with it. Many animals can come partly out of their shells, and some even have 'doors' that can be closed for safety. As a snail grows, its shell grows bigger too, so that there is more room inside. Spiral snail shells nearly all twist the same way. If you look at the point of the shell and follow the spiral outwards, it goes clockwise.

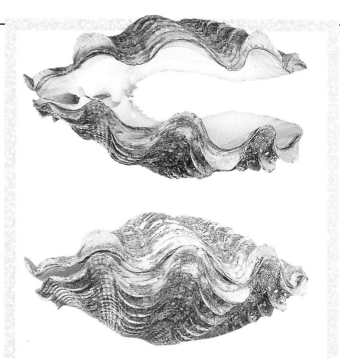

Clams have two half-shells hinged together. When danger threatens, they are held tightly closed by a strong muscle.

Shell stone

Animals that live in the sea take calcium carbonate from the water and gradually build up their shells with it. Shells can be a variety of different shapes and sizes. Millions of years ago, the shells of dead animals settled in thick layers at the bottom of the sea. Gradually, the shells were squashed together to become rock.

The shell of a Roman snail is a coiled tube. As the snail grows it adds to the tube, making it longer and wider.

14

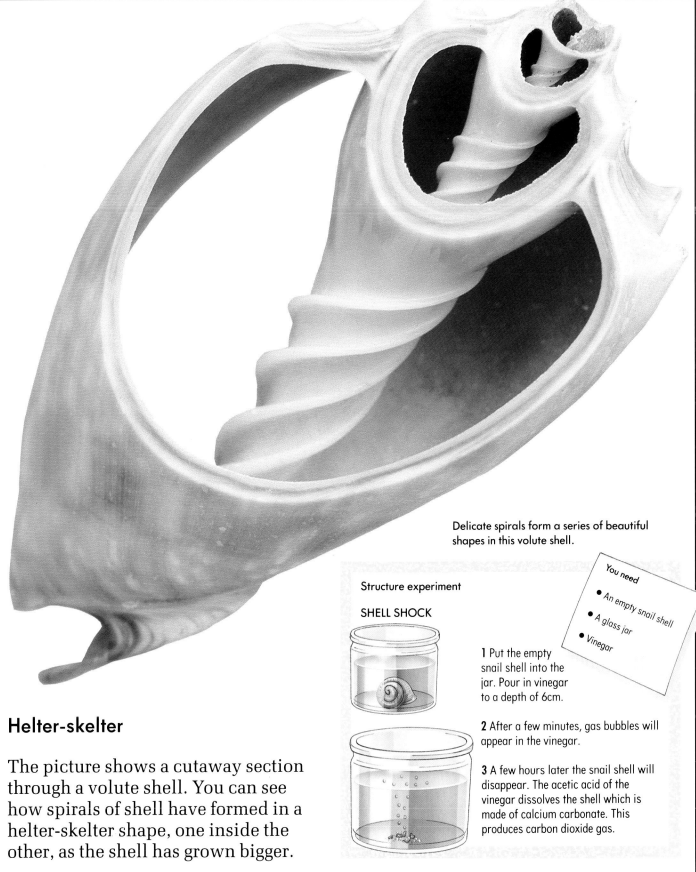

Delicate spirals form a series of beautiful shapes in this volute shell.

Helter-skelter

The picture shows a cutaway section through a volute shell. You can see how spirals of shell have formed in a helter-skelter shape, one inside the other, as the shell has grown bigger.

Structure experiment

SHELL SHOCK

You need

• An empty snail shell

• A glass jar

• Vinegar

1 Put the empty snail shell into the jar. Pour in vinegar to a depth of 6cm.

2 After a few minutes, gas bubbles will appear in the vinegar.

3 A few hours later the snail shell will disappear. The acetic acid of the vinegar dissolves the shell which is made of calcium carbonate. This produces carbon dioxide gas.

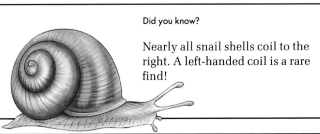

Did you know?

Nearly all snail shells coil to the right. A left-handed coil is a rare find!

Joints and levers

It is very important for a living creature to have a rigid skeleton that supports and protects the soft parts of its body. But, to move about, a skeleton must be jointed. There are two main sorts of **joints** – hinged joints and ball joints. Hinged joints allow only backward and forward movement. Your knee is a hinged joint. The lower part of your leg will move only back and forth. Your hip is a ball joint that lets you move your thigh around.

Hinge and ball

This picture shows a rabbit's ankle and knee joints, which are hinges. They bend backwards and forwards.

Levering along

Rowing oars are **levers**. As you pull on them, they turn in the rowlocks fixed to the sides of the boat and the blades push against the water, forcing the boat forwards. The fixed point around which a lever turns is called its **fulcrum**. So each rowlock is a fulcrum. The distance from your hands to the rowlocks is shorter than the distance from the rowlocks to the blades of the oars. A short, slow movement of your hands makes a longer, faster movement of the blades.

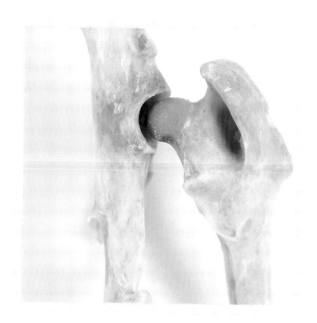

A rabbit's hip is a ball joint. The ball on the thigh bone (on the right) fits snugly into the hip socket.

Structure experiment

BALANCING THE MONEY!

1 Put the pencil on a table and balance the ruler over it at the centre mark (fulcrum).

2 Put one coin on the ruler at the 17cm mark. Where must you put the other coin to make the ruler balance again?

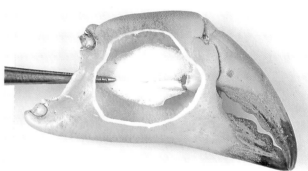

3 Now put a second coin on top of the first. Where do you have to put the third coin to balance the ruler?

4 Experiment with different weights (numbers of coins) at different distances from the fulcrum.

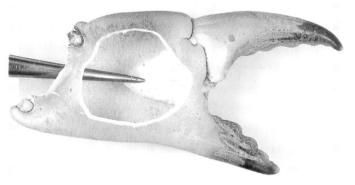

Crabby crunch

In the pictures above, a crab's claw is cut away to show how it works. The moving part of the claw is an L-shaped lever with its fulcrum at the angle of the L. When the muscle pulls on the flat white piece inside, the claw starts to close. In the picture, the metal tweezers are acting as the muscle. As they pull the claw shut, you can see where the flat white piece is attached to the bony claw.

Tubes

Animals and plants are full of hollow tubes of various kinds. Soft flexible tubes carry liquid like blood around an animal's body, or pump sap into the leaves of plants. Rigid tubes form the skeletons of many animals. Most bones are rigid tubes with soft marrow inside. The legs of insects and crabs are covered with tubes of chitin. Hollow tubes are much stronger than solid rods of the same weight.

Light and rigid

Bird bones must be light and strong, otherwise it would be difficult for large birds, like this gannet, to fly. Tubes are both light and strong.

Soft tubes

Blood is taken around your body by a network of flexible tubes. The heart pumps blood into tubes called **arteries**. These branch out to all parts of the body. The blood then travels back to the heart by similar tubes called veins. There are also tubes inside you which carry food through your body, and air tubes for breathing. The air tubes leading to your lungs have strong rings all the way down them to keep them open when you suck in air.

The artery running up the middle of this rabbit's ear branches out, taking blood to all parts of the ear. The vein running down the edge collects the used blood and takes it back to the heart.

A section through a wing-bone.

Frigate birds spend nearly all their time gliding high above the oceans. Their light wing-bones are nothing more than thin tubes.

Structure experiment

WHICH IS STRONGER – TUBE OR ROD?

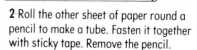

1 Roll up one sheet of paper tightly into a solid rod. Fasten it together with sticky tape.

2 Roll the other sheet of paper round a pencil to make a tube. Fasten it together with sticky tape. Remove the pencil.

3 Put the bricks about 13cm apart. Rest the paper rod and tube 5cm apart on the bricks. Place the flower pot over the tube and rod. Add stones to the pot until one of the paper supports bends.

You need
- Two bricks
- Two sheets of A4 paper
- A 12cm plastic flower pot
- Some stones
- Sticky tape

Tubes for strength

Bicycles are made of steel tubes, each about 28mm in diameter. The tubes are joined together to make a frame that is rigid and very strong. But the metal from which tubes are made is less than 1mm thick. If the tubes were melted down and formed into solid rods, these would measure only 7mm across. A bicycle made from 7mm rods would weigh the same as a normal bike but would bend and buckle if you tried to ride it.

The frame on this stunt bike needs to be strong. It is made of tubular steel.

Teeth and horns

Animals' bones are strong and hard but their teeth are even harder. They contain enamel, the toughest material made in an animal's body. Teeth need to be hard, so that they do not wear away too fast when animals chew their food. Horns are also made of hard material. Deer antlers are solid bone, but hollow cow horns are made from layers of hard **keratin**, and grow over a core of bone. Insects like beetles have horns of hard chitin.

The front teeth of this beaver have a thick layer of orange enamel. They wear away at an angle, leaving a sharp edge.

Tooth or tusk?

Tusks are extra long teeth. Elephants use their tusks to uproot trees or to lever off the bark. They eat leafy twigs and bark which they chew up with huge, flat **molar** teeth. Elephant's molars are made of many layers of enamel sandwiched between layers of **dentine**, which is a hard form of bone. The ridges of enamel are good for grinding up food.

Elephants' tusks are extra-long teeth. They use them to strip the bark from trees.

20

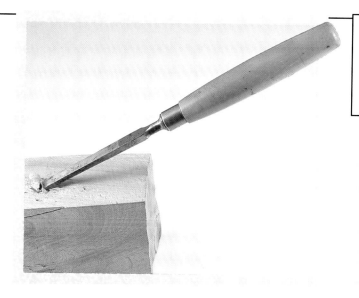

Sharpening a chisel makes it shorter. Beavers sharpen their teeth but, as the teeth grow all the time, they never get shorter.

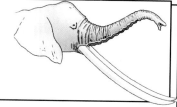

Did you know?

The longest elephant tusk known was 3.5 metres long.

Structure experiment

DON'T BITE OFF MORE THAN YOU CAN CHEW!

1 Bite off a piece of apple and chew it up completely.

2 Repeat this, using only your front teeth to *chew* as well as bite.

3 Try it again, using only your back teeth to *bite* as well as chew.

Which teeth are best for biting and which for grinding?

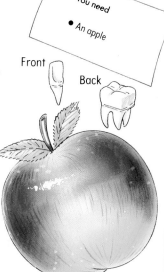

You need
● An apple

Front

Back

Hair or horn?

Cow horns are hollow. Long ago, people used them as drinking cups, or as hunting horns to signal to each other. The strong hollow horns fit snugly onto spikes of bone on the cow's skull. A rhinoceros horn is solid, but it is not made of bone. Instead, the horn is made of fibres, like hairs, packed together. Some people think that the ground-up horn is a powerful medicine.

This is an African black rhinoceros. It uses the two horns on its snout to defend itself against enemies.

Jaws and beaks

You can sometimes tell what food an animal eats by the sort of jaws or beak it has. Fish-eating birds may have sharp, straight beaks for darting at fish. Nectar-sucking birds have long, thin beaks that fit deep inside flowers. But jaws and beaks are not just for feeding with. They can also be used for fighting, or as tools. A bird can use its beak to weave twigs carefully into a nest.

The strong, sharp blades of these secateurs easily slice through wood. A parrot uses its beak to slice up its food in a similar way.

Horny beaks

Birds' beaks are made rather like cows' horns. There is a horny layer that fits over solid bone. Many birds' beaks grow all through their lives, and so have to be worn away. Starlings' beaks grow fast, but are quickly worn away as they poke them into the ground to find worms and grubs. Birds use their beaks as tools. A woodpecker's beak is like a hammer and chisel all in one. A wren's beak is like fine tweezers for picking spiders out of cracks in bark.

A macaw's beak is strong enough to crack a nut but it can use it daintily to straighten a ruffled feather.

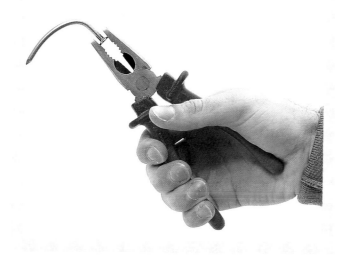

An animal's jaws are a bit like a pair of pliers. Animals use their jaws for holding things, as well as for chewing their food.

Structure experiment

A GRAIN OF TRUTH!

Imagine the tweezers, secateurs and scissors are different kinds of beak.

1 Try picking up a rice grain with the tweezers, secateurs and scissors in turn. Which picks up the rice most easily?

2 Look at the beak shapes of some of the birds in the park, or garden. Can you guess what food each bird eats? Check your answer with a reference book.

You need
- A few rice grains
- Tweezers
- Scissors
- Secateurs

Jaws of chitin

Insects' jaws are hard and strong. The larvae of furniture beetles and death-watch beetles make little holes in dead wood. Carpenter bees, which are like big bumble bees, also bore holes in wood with their jaws. Caterpillars use their strong jaws to chew up leaves. Spiders and centipedes do not have jaws, but thin, curved poison fangs. The bite of a black widow spider is as dangerous as a snake bite.

A stag beetle closes its jaws as it takes off. Males use their jaws for fighting.

Spines and scales

Animals have spines and scales for protection. Scales provide a hard, outer layer rather like the outer skeleton of an insect. But there is an important difference. An insect's armour bends only at the joints while a lizard's scales slide over each other so that it can bend its body in any direction. Spines can injure an attacker. A leopard that tries to catch a porcupine may get its paws full of long quills.

Space scales

This space shuttle has a covering of hard, tough tiles. They protect it from damage when it returns to Earth.

Pointing prickles

Animals and plants have spines for protection. Some sea urchins have long needle-sharp spines of calcium carbonate. Just touching one spine with your finger makes all the other spines around it move towards your finger. Nothing gets close to a sea urchin without being pricked. The spines are so sharp that, if you tread on them, they can pass right through the rubber sole of a shoe and stick into your foot.

This hedgehog is sitting among brambles. When there is danger, it can roll itself into a tight ball of prickly spines.

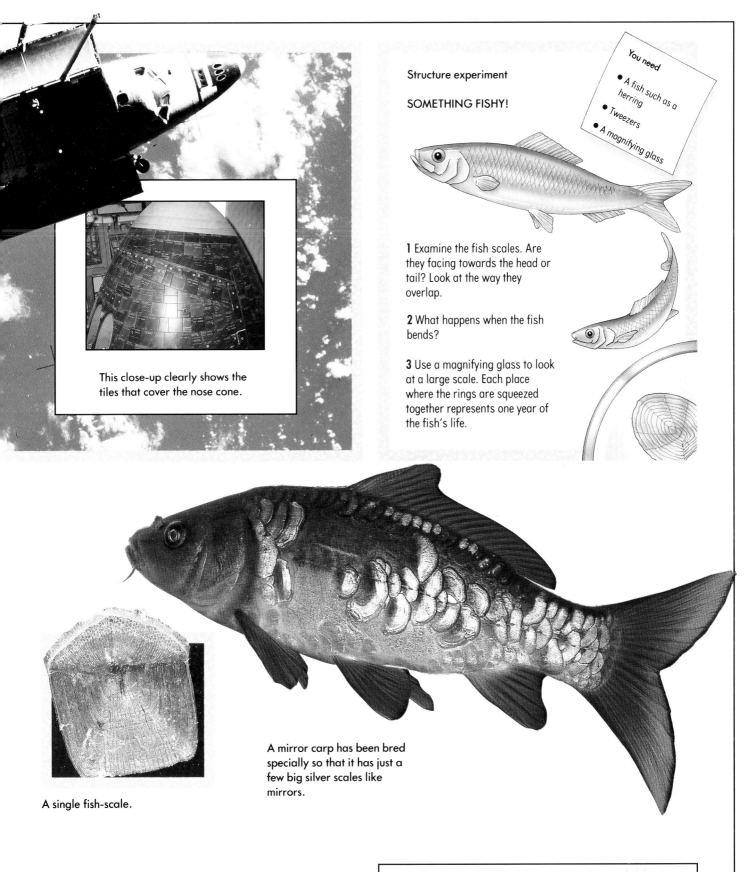

This close-up clearly shows the tiles that cover the nose cone.

Structure experiment

SOMETHING FISHY!

1 Examine the fish scales. Are they facing towards the head or tail? Look at the way they overlap.

2 What happens when the fish bends?

3 Use a magnifying glass to look at a large scale. Each place where the rings are squeezed together represents one year of the fish's life.

A single fish-scale.

A mirror carp has been bred specially so that it has just a few big silver scales like mirrors.

Most fish have a layer of protective scales. The scales are slimy, to help the fish move through the water and for protection against disease.

Did you know?

The hedgehog's spines are springy, so it does not hurt itself if it falls onto its back from a height!

Fur and feather

Scaly animals, like fish and lizards, **evolved** many millions of years ago. Animals with fur and feathers evolved later. Unlike scales, fur and feathers are not for protection, but make good **insulation**. A warm layer of soft **down** under a rough outer coat keeps an animal's body warm. Animals with fur or feathers are warm-blooded and have more energy than cold-blooded animals. They can run or fly away fast from enemies, and do not need to be protected by heavy scales.

Like fur and feathers, a snow-suit has a weatherproof outer layer with soft insulating material underneath. These snow-suits keep the children warm and dry.

Trapped warmth

Mammals have hair on their bodies. Fur is lots of hairs growing close together. The hairs grow out of the skin at an angle, so that they all lie in the same direction. Each hair has a tiny muscle attached to its base. When it is cold, these muscles pull all the hairs upright. When fur is standing on end, it traps the air next to the skin, keeping the body warmer.

This dormouse's fur keeps it warm while it **hibernates** to escape the winter cold.

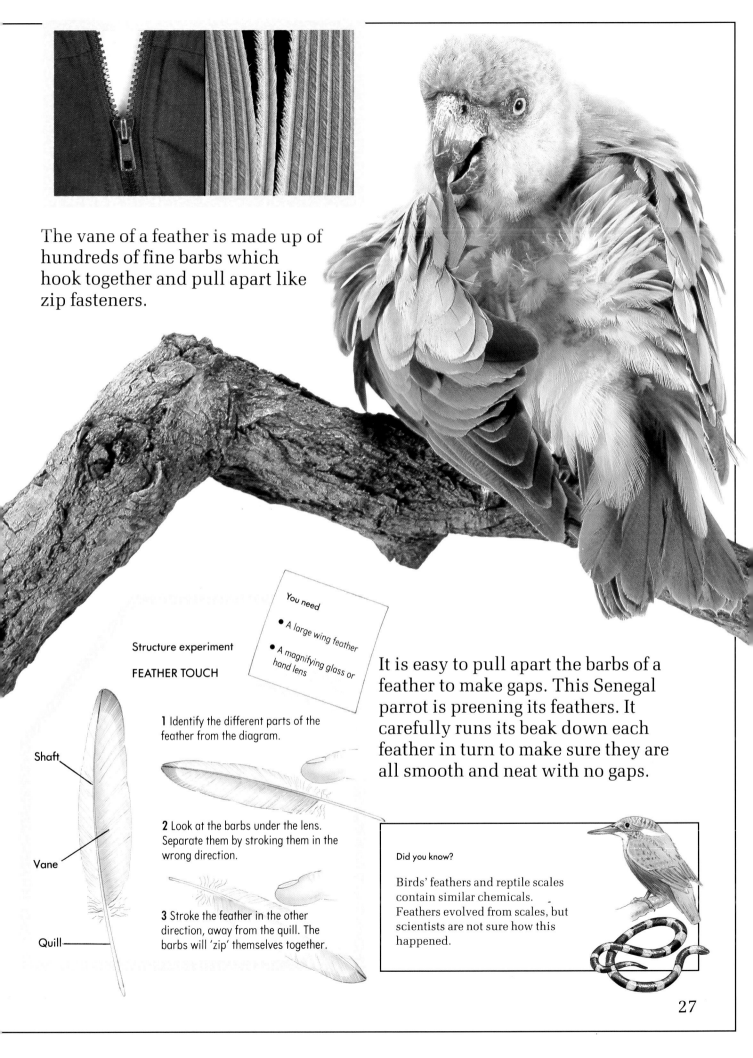

The vane of a feather is made up of hundreds of fine barbs which hook together and pull apart like zip fasteners.

You need

● A large wing feather

● A magnifying glass or hand lens

Structure experiment

FEATHER TOUCH

1 Identify the different parts of the feather from the diagram.

2 Look at the barbs under the lens. Separate them by stroking them in the wrong direction.

3 Stroke the feather in the other direction, away from the quill. The barbs will 'zip' themselves together.

Shaft

Vane

Quill

It is easy to pull apart the barbs of a feather to make gaps. This Senegal parrot is preening its feathers. It carefully runs its beak down each feather in turn to make sure they are all smooth and neat with no gaps.

Did you know?

Birds' feathers and reptile scales contain similar chemicals. Feathers evolved from scales, but scientists are not sure how this happened.

27

Wings

Insects were the first animals on Earth to fly. Birds came later, and later still came bats. All these animals have wings which are made up of stiff struts supporting a thin covering to trap the air. The struts of a bat's wing are the bones of its arms and fingers; the thin covering is skin. The struts of a bird's wing are the shafts of its feathers as well as the bones of its arms, while insect wings have struts made of chitin.

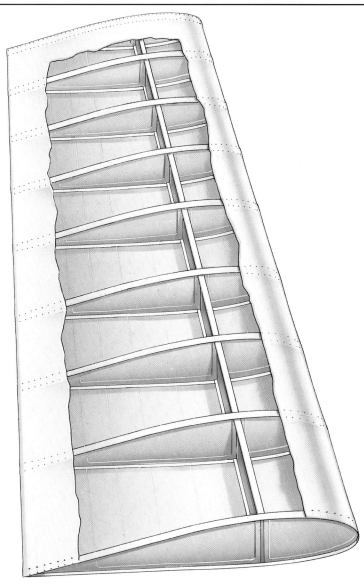

An aircraft wing has a thin covering on the outside supported by a strong inner framework.

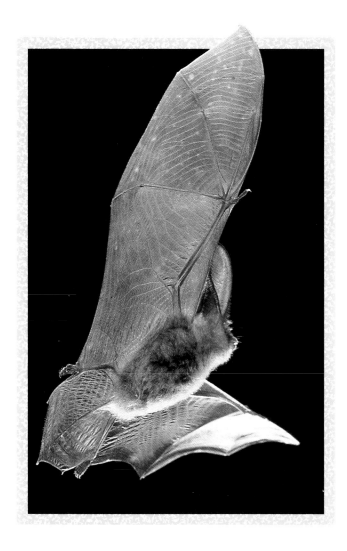

Stretchy wings

A bat's wings are made of thin skin stretched over the bones of its arms and fingers. Its thumbs are like hooks, and can be used for climbing or handling food. The skin is stretchy and folds up easily when the bat lands. Bats have little bodies and big wings. They cannot fly as fast as birds but they can dart about and change direction quickly in a way that birds find difficult.

The wing of a hang glider is made of metal struts supporting a thin sheet of material. It is rather like a bat's wing.

Hang glider

The wings of this hang glider are similar to a bat's wings. A thin sheet of very light material is stretched tightly over a framework of strong aluminium struts. The hang glider pilot rides high in the air on warm air currents which keep him or her up. To steer the hang glider, the pilot uses a control bar and his or her body movements. Some hang gliders, known as powered hang gliders, are fitted with a small engine.

Structure experiment
MAKE A DELTA WING

1 Divide the paper in half with a ruled pencil line.

2 Rule lines from one end of the centre line to the furthest corners. Cut along the lines to make a delta shape.

3 Cut 3 balsa wood struts to fit the wing shape. Glue them across the centre line as shown.

4 Glue the remaining piece of balsa stick across the struts along the centre line.

5 Stick a lump of Plasticine about the size of a marble on the nose of the delta wing. You will have to adjust the weight of the Plasticine to make the wing fly smoothly.

You need

- A sheet of A4 paper
- A pencil
- A ruler
- Scissors
- Glue
- A stick of balsa wood 4×4mm, 805mm long
- A craft knife
- Plasticine

Building

Like humans, some animals build homes for themselves. They know just what materials to use and how to join them together. Birds make nests by wedging twigs and other materials into the fork of a tree, or by sticking mud on to the side of a cliff. Honeybees build nests out of wax, and wasps make paper nests from wood. Ants are also good nest-builders, using soil stuck together with saliva.

Building a high-rise office block.

Heavy construction

The houses that people live in are usually built of brick, wood, or stone. Large buildings such as schools, hospitals and factories are usually made of concrete, a much stronger material. Some of the buildings made by human beings are so big that they will not stand up without some extra support. The biggest buildings are held up by metal girders set into concrete supports. The biggest animal buildings are termite hills, which can be as high as 3 metres.

Structure experiment

IT'S A WASPS' NEST!

1 Blow up the balloon and tie the end.

2 Tear off squares of newspaper about 5cm × 5cm. Cover the balloon with overlapping layers of paper squares, sticking them with glue. Leave the knot uncovered.

3 Leave the 'nest' to dry overnight. Untie the knot and pull out the balloon.

Wasps gathering round the entrance to their nest.

Did you know?

The world's tallest building is the Sears Tower in Chicago, USA. It is 443 metres high.

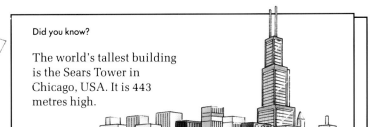

Cell layers

Inside a wasps' nest, the cells are built in layers like the floors in a block of flats. Each layer of cells is separated from the rest by rigid struts. Hundreds of wasp grubs hang in the cells.

Structure words

Arteries Tubes that carry blood from the heart around the body.

Atom The smallest piece of an element.

Calcium carbonate The chemical name for chalk.

Carbon An element that is in all living things, and forms soot and diamonds.

Chitin The tough material that forms the outer skeleton of insects and animals such as crabs.

Compression A force that pushes.

Crystal A solid with its atoms arranged in a regular pattern.

Dentine The hard material that teeth are made from.

Down A soft feather layer next to a bird's skin.

Evaporate To change from a liquid into a vapour.

Evolve To develop slowly over millions of years.

Fulcrum The point around which a lever turns.

Insulation Material that stops a body losing warmth.

Joint Where two or more bones connect.

Keratin The material from which horn is made.

Lever A long straight bar that turns on a fulcrum and can be used to move a heavy load.

Ligaments Tough cords in the body that join bones and muscles.

Microscopic Something so small that it can only be seen clearly through a microscope.

Molar A large, flat grinding tooth.

Molecule The smallest part of a compound.

Muscles The parts of a human or animal body that contract and relax to make the body move.

Nucleus The control-centre of a cell.

Silica The chemical name for sand and glass.

Solution Any substance dissolved in a liquid.

Tension A force that pulls.

Index

PICTURE CREDITS

All photographs are by Kim Taylor and Jane Burton except for those supplied by The Research House/NASA 24-25 (top); ZEFA 3, 8-9 (below), 10-11, 13 (below), 16 (below), 19 (below), 20 (top), 25 (top), 26 (top), 29.